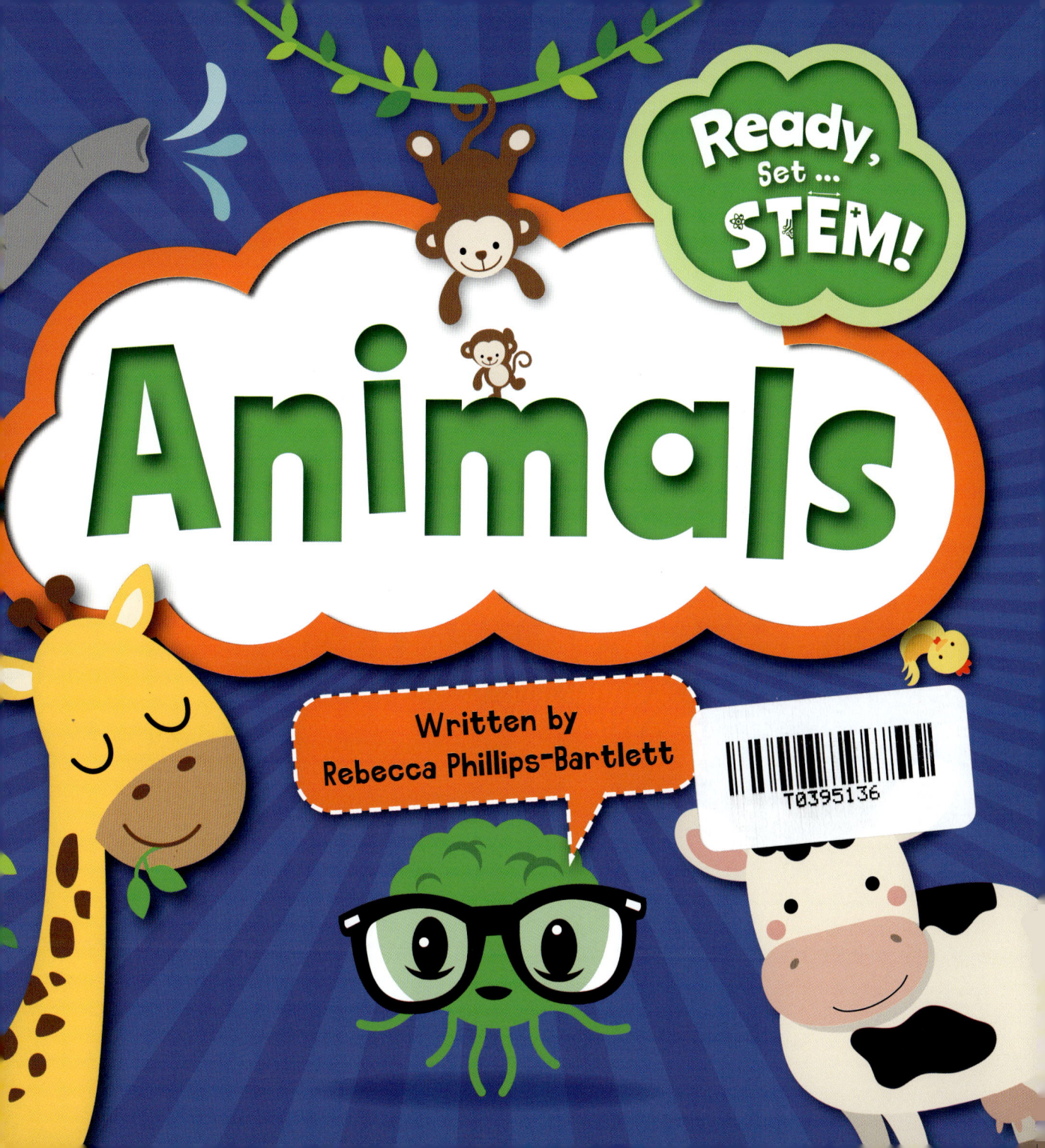

Animals

Written by
Rebecca Phillips-Bartlett

Ready, Set ... STEM!

Library of Congress Control Number:
The Library of Congress Control Number is available on the Library of Congress website.

ISBN
979-8-89359-289-4 (library bound)
979-8-89359-294-8 (paperback)
979-8-89359-303-7 (epub)
979-8-89359-299-3 (hosted ebook)

Printed in the United States of America
Mankato, MN

012025

Written by:
Rebecca Phillips-Bartlett
Edited by:
Noah Leatherland
Designed by:
Amelia Harris

All facts, statistics, web addresses and URLs in this book were verified as valid and accurate at time of writing. No responsibility for any changes to external websites or references can be accepted by either the author or publisher.

Photo Credits

Contents

Words that look like this can be found in the glossary on page 24.

Animals Around Us

Hi, everyone! I'm Brain the brian. Wait, that doesn't sound right. I'm Brian the brain. Yes, that's better. I'm always getting those words mixed up! Let's learn about animals together!

HELLO! My name is
~~Brain~~ Brian
(the brain)

Animals, including humans, are living things. They need air, food, and water to live. What other things do humans need to live?

Ready, Set ... THINK!

5

Types of Animals

There are many different types of animals. Animals can be big or small. Some animals are fluffy. Others might be scaly, slimy, or feathery.

Think about your favorite animal. How would you describe it?

Animals live in many different places, from down in the ground to high up in the trees. Go for a walk outside with an adult. How many animals can you count?

Ready, Set ... COUNT!

So Many Mammals

Mammals are a type of warm-blooded animal. All mammals have hair and a backbone. Mammals make milk to feed their babies.

Mammals breathe using <u>organs</u> called lungs. When you breathe, your tummy moves as your lungs fill with air. Put your hand gently on your tummy.

Ready, Set ... BREATHE!

Did you feel your tummy move?

9

Beautiful Birds

Like mammals, all birds are warm-blooded and have a backbone. However, birds also have feathers, wings, and a beak. All birds lay eggs.

Not all birds can fly! Penguins and ostriches are <u>flightless</u> birds.

10

Feathers help birds stay warm and dry. Some birds use their feathers to show off or to hide. Go on a wildlife walk. See how many feathers you can spot!

Ready, Set ... SEARCH!

Can you hear any birds tweeting?

Fantastic Fish

Fish are a fantastic type of animal! Fish live in water. They breathe using a body part called gills. Most fish are covered in smooth, tough scales.

Some fish live in saltwater seas. Others live in fresh water, such as in rivers or ponds.

Fish do not have legs. They swim using fins. One of the fastest fish in the world is called a sailfish. Can you swim as fast as a sailfish?

Ready, Set ... SWIM!

13

Remarkable Reptiles

Reptiles, such as snakes and crocodiles, have dry, scaly skin. Reptiles are cold-blooded. This means they cannot warm themselves up or cool themselves down without help.

14

Crocodiles live near water. If they need to cool down, they go for a splash in the water. Crocodiles have strong, snapping <u>jaws</u>. Can you snap your arms like a crocodile's jaw?

Ready, Set ... SNAP!

Snap! Snap! Snap!

15

Amazing Amphibians

Amphibians are cold-blooded animals. They can live on land or in the water. Amphibians lay eggs. When young amphibians <u>hatch</u> from their eggs, they have gills. As they get older, they grow lungs.

16

Frogs and toads are both amphibians. Toads have dry, warty skin and short legs. Frogs have smooth, slimy skin and long legs.

1.

? Which of these is a toad and which is a frog?

2.

Ready, Set ... SPOT THE DIFFERENCE!

Incredible Invertebrates

Invertebrates are around us all the time. Insects, spiders, snails, and worms are all types of invertebrates. Invertebrates do not have backbones.

Most of the world's animals are invertebrates.

18

Some invertebrates, such as snails, have shells to keep them safe. Some invertebrates' bodies are covered with a hard outer layer called an exoskeleton. Next time you are outside, look out for invertebrates.

Ready, Set ... LOOK!

19

Create Your Own

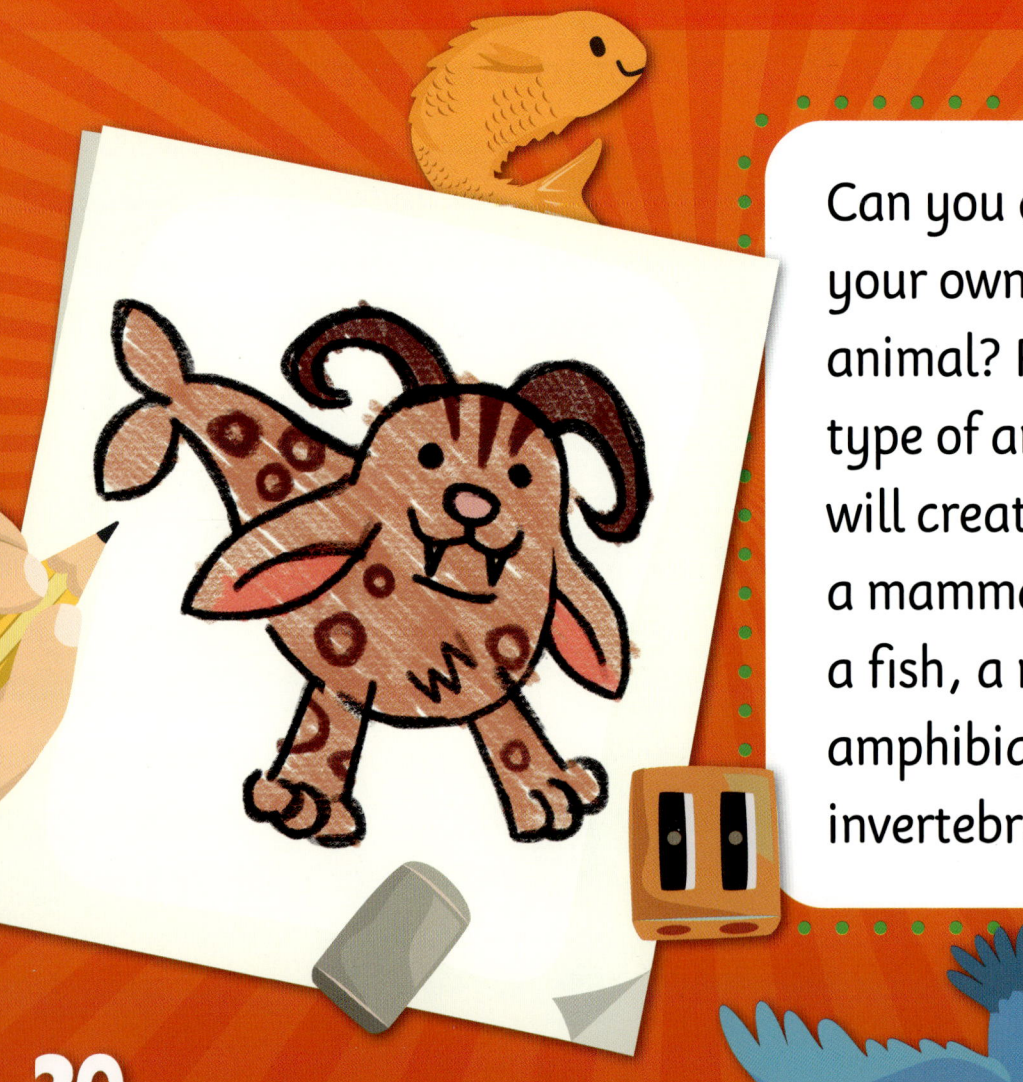

Can you create your own amazing animal? Pick the type of animal you will create. Will it be a mammal, a bird, a fish, a reptile, an amphibian, or an invertebrate?

Grab your paper and some pencils. Then, create a new animal.

Does your animal have legs, wings, fins, or all three?

Does it have fur, scales, or feathers?

What color is your creature?

Ready, Set ... DRAW!

21

Take a Trip

We share the world with so many animals. Why not take a trip with an adult to see some of the incredible creatures we live with?

Whether you wander through the woods or peer inside the pond, there are many animals to discover!

Make sure you do not disturb the animals you find.

Ready, Set ... EXPLORE!

23

Glossary

describe   to say what something is like

flightless   unable to fly

hatch   when a young animal comes out of its egg

jaws   the upper and lower part of the mouth containing the teeth

organs   body parts that have specific, important jobs to do

Index